EARLY PRAISE

for

THE OFFICIAL BITCOIN COLORING BOOK

"There is nothing I enjoy better than lounging in my silk robe with a tumbler of 18 year old Lephraud single malt and *The Official Bitcoin Coloring Book*. I do the actually coloring work of course, while my young (ahem) assistant keeps a disciplined eye on my progress. She makes darned sure I stay well within the lines. And do I ever. Absolutely intoxicating."
—**Diamond James**, CEO, J.P. Morgain

"I'm a huge fan of Satoshi's work, especially his new *Official Bitcoin Coloring Book*, and I think it's a must for everyone in the crypto space. I bought a copy, then eye-scanned it and cached in my visual cortex. I do the coloring work virtually, in the background. I like how it frees that part of my brain from distractions, so I can focus on the important stuff like scaling Etheorum better and making it even more difficult to understand. But that's just me."
—**Vitallike Buttering**, programming wunderkind and creator of the Etheorum blockchain platform

"Everyone knows I built my fortune by reading boring footnotes in boring financial reports, and making boring investments in boring companies. It's taken a long boring lifetime, but it has finally paid off. Now, other people spend hours reading my boring footnotes. And some even pay millions to watch me eat lunch and bore them about topics like compound interest. So this Bitcoin business really gets my goat. Some of these young fellows are getting very rich, very fast, without being boring at all. It irks me. Especially the Lambos. I've always secretly wanted one, but when your whole life is predicated on being dull and folksy, well, a Huracán Performante is just not an option. So *The Official Bitcoin Coloring Book* has been a godsend for me. I work on it privately in my wood-paneled den and daydream about a different life, away from pinstriped suits and actuarial tables. And I'm not usually one to boast, but I have gotten pretty good at this coloring business. Right now, I'm sticking with the one color I know best—grey. But soon . . ."
—**Buffet Warden**, billionaire investor and Chairman of the Bored, Blandshire Haffling

THE OFFICIAL
BITCOIN
COLORING BOOK

The Official Bitcoin Coloring Book
Copyright © 2019 by Satoshi Nakamoto

Published by
LEAF STORM PRESS
Post Office Box 4670
Santa Fe, New Mexico 87502
U.S.A.
leafstormpress.com

Cover image: 123rf © Lukas Gojda Interior: 123rf © Ievgen Radchenko P7 | © William
Roberts P25 | © Gal Amar P59 | © Vera Petruk P71 | dreamstime © Natasha7409 P33 |
© Ekaterina Glazovak P35 | © Viktoriia Panchenko P39 | © Creativehearts P51
| illustrations © anon PG 21, 23, 43, 49 | graphic design by anon

Leaf Storm logos are trademarks of Leaf Storm Press LLC.

To inquire about bulk discounts for special events, promotions and premiums
please contact the publisher by email at leafstormpress@gmail.com.

First edition.
Printed in the U.S.A.
Book Design by LSP Graphics
SPPC-7413596629

Library of Progress
Cataloguing In Publication Data is available

ISBN 978-1-9456520-1-1

THE OFFICIAL
BITCOIN
COLORING BOOK

SATOSHI NAKAMOTO

LeafStormPress

SANTA FE, NEW MEXICO

THE FINE PRINT AT THE BOTTOM OF THE PAGE

The #1 selling brand

SIMPLY THE BEST

Keep it Handy!

Occam's* razor

GETS SHARPER WITH DAILY USE!

Proven and effective relief from:

- complexplanation
- conspiracy theories
- indecisiveness
- mental clutter
- distraction
- designer stubble

It does not matter how slowly you go as long as you do not stop.
—CONFUCIUS

FORTIS FORTUNA ADIUVAT

Bitcoin: A Peer-to-Peer Electronic Cash System

Abstract. A purely peer-to-peer version of electronic cash would allow online payments to be sent directly from one party to another without going through a financial institution. Digital signatures provide part of the solution, but the main benefits are lost if a trusted third party is still required to prevent double-spending. We propose a solution to the double-spending problem using a peer-to-peer network. The network timestamps transactions by hashing them into an ongoing chain of hash-based proof-of-work, forming a record that cannot be changed without redoing the proof-of-work. The longest chain not only serves as proof of the sequence of events witnessed, but proof that it came from the largest pool of CPU power. As long as a majority of CPU power is controlled by nodes that are not cooperating to attack the network, they'll generate the longest chain and outpace attackers. The network itself requires minimal structure. Messages are broadcast on a best effort basis, and nodes can leave and rejoin the network at will, accepting the longest proof-of-work chain as proof of what happened while they were gone.

1. Introduction

Commerce on the Internet has come to rely almost exclusively on financial institutions serving as trusted third parties to process electronic payments. While the system works well enough for most transactions, it still suffers from

WORLD BANKING 2008

the inherent weaknesses of the trust-based model. Completely non-reversible transactions are not really possible, since financial institutions cannot avoid mediating disputes. The cost of mediation increases transaction costs, limiting the minimum practical transaction size and cutting off the possibility for small casual transactions, and there is a broader cost in the loss of ability to make non-reversible payments for non-reversible services. With the possibility of reversal, the need for trust spreads. Merchants must be wary of their customers, hassling them for more information than they would otherwise need. A certain percentage of fraud is accepted as unavoidable. These costs and payment uncertainties can be avoided in person by using physical currency, but no mechanism exists to make payments over a communications channel without a trusted party.

What is needed is an electronic payment system based on cryptographic proof instead of trust, allowing any two willing parties to transact directly with each other without the need for a trusted third party. Transactions that are computationally impractical to reverse would protect sellers from fraud, and routine escrow mechanisms could easily be implemented to protect buyers. In this paper, we propose a solution to the double-spending problem using a peer-to-peer distributed timestamp server to generate

ANCIENT MONEY

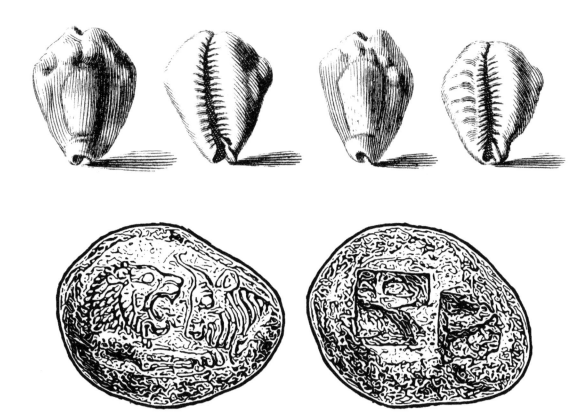

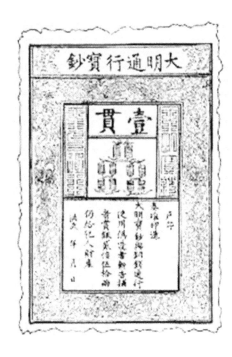

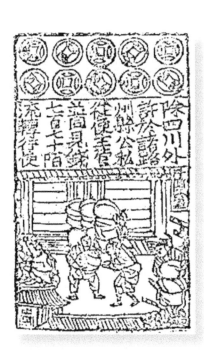

computational proof of the chronological order of transactions. The system is secure as long as honest nodes collectively control more CPU power than any cooperating group of attacker nodes.

2. Transactions

We define an electronic coin as a chain of digital signatures. Each owner transfers the coin to the next by digitally signing a hash of the previous transaction and the public key of the next owner and adding these to the end of the coin. A payee can verify the signatures to verify the chain of ownership.

OLD MONEY

The problem of course is the payee can't verify that one of the owners did not double spend the coin. A common solution is to introduce a trusted central authority, or mint, that checks every transaction for double spending. After each transaction, the coin must be returned to the mint to issue a new coin, and only coins issued directly from the mint are trusted not to be double spent. The problem with this solution is that the fate of the entire money system depends on the company running the mint, with every transaction having to go through them, just like a bank.

We need a way for the payee to know that the previous owners did not sign any earlier transactions. For our purposes, the earliest transaction is the one that counts, so we don't care about later attempts to double-spend. The only way to confirm the absence of a transaction is to be aware of all transactions. In the mint based model, the mint was aware of all transactions and decided which arrived first. To accomplish this without a trusted party, transactions must be publicly announced [1], and we need a system for participants to agree on a single history of the order in which they were received. The payee needs proof that at the time of each transaction, the majority of nodes agreed it was the first received.

PRESENT DAY

MAJOR FIAT CURRENCIES

3. Timestamp Server

The solution we propose begins with a timestamp server. A timestamp server works by taking a hash of a block of items to be time-stamped and widely publishing the hash, such as in a newspaper or Usenet post [2-5]. The timestamp proves that the data must have existed at the time, obviously, in order to get into the hash. Each timestamp includes the previous timestamp in its hash, forming a chain, with each additional timestamp reinforcing the ones before it.

4. Proof-of-Work

To implement a distributed timestamp server on a peer-to-peer basis, we will need to use a proof-of-work system similar to Adam Back's Hashcash [6], rather than newspaper or Usenet posts. The proof-of-work involves scanning for a value that when hashed, such as with SHA-256, the hash begins with a number of zero bits. The average work required is exponential in the number of zero bits required and can be verified by executing a single hash.

LEGACY BANKING

For our timestamp network, we implement the proof-of-work by incrementing a nonce in the block until a value is found that gives the block's hash the required zero bits. Once the CPU effort has been expended to make it satisfy the proof-of-work, the block cannot be changed without redoing the work. As later blocks are chained after it, the work to change the block would include redoing all the blocks after it.

The proof-of-work also solves the problem of determining representation in majority decision-making. If the majority were based on one-IP-address-one-vote, it could be subverted by anyone able to allocate many IPs. Proof-of-work is essentially one-CPU-one-vote. The majority decision is represented by the longest chain, which has the greatest proof-of-work effort invested in it. If a majority of CPU power is controlled by honest nodes, the honest chain will

grow the fastest and outpace any competing chains. To modify a past block, an attacker would have to redo the proof-of-work of the block and all blocks after it and then catch up with and surpass the work of the honest nodes. We will show later that the probability of a slower attacker catching up diminishes exponentially as subsequent blocks are added.

To compensate for increasing hardware speed and varying interest in running nodes over time, the proof-of-work difficulty is determined by a moving average targeting an average number of blocks per hour. If they're generated too fast, the difficulty increases.

5. Network

The steps to run the network are as follows:

1) New transactions are broadcast to all nodes.
2) Each node collects new transactions into a block.
3) Each node works on finding a difficult proof-of-work for its block.
4) When a node finds a proof-of-work, it broadcasts the block to all nodes.
5) Nodes accept the block only if all transactions in it are valid and not already spent.

OUT OF THIN AIR

6) Nodes express their acceptance of the block by working on creating the next block in the chain, using the hash of the accepted block as the previous hash.

Nodes always consider the longest chain to be the correct one and will keep working on extending it. If two nodes broadcast different versions of the next block simultaneously, some nodes may receive one or the other first. In that case, they work on the first one they received, but save the other branch in case it becomes longer. The tie will be broken when the next proof-of-work is found and one branch becomes longer; the nodes that were working on the other branch will then switch to the longer one.

New transaction broadcasts do not necessarily need to reach all nodes. As long as they reach many nodes, they will get into a block before long. Block broadcasts are also tolerant of dropped messages. If a node does not receive a block, it will request it when it receives the next block and realizes it missed one.

6. Incentive
By convention, the first transaction in a block is a special transaction that starts a new coin owned by the creator of the block. This adds an incentive for nodes to support the network, and provides a way to initially distribute coins

into circulation, since there is no central authority to issue them. The steady addition of a constant of amount of new coins is analogous to gold miners expending resources to add gold to circulation. In our case, it is CPU time and electricity that is expended.

The incentive can also be funded with transaction fees. If the output value of a transaction is less than its input value, the difference is a transaction fee that is added to the incentive value of the block containing the transaction. Once a predetermined number of coins have entered circulation, the incentive can transition entirely to transaction fees and be completely inflation free.

The incentive may help encourage nodes to stay honest. If a greedy attacker is able to assemble more CPU power than all the honest nodes, he would have to choose between using it to defraud people by stealing back his payments, or using it to generate new coins. He ought to find it more profitable to play by the rules, such rules that favour him with more new coins than everyone else combined, than to undermine the system and the validity of his own wealth.

THE
BLOCK
OF
GENESIS

```
00000000
00000010  f9 be b4 d9 1d 01 00 00   01 00 00 00 00 00 00 00   |...............|
00000020  00 00 00 00 00 00 00 00   00 00 00 00 00 00 00 00   |...............|
00000030  00 00 00 00 00 00 00 00   00 00 00 00 3b a3 ed fd   |............;...|
00000040  7a 7b 12 b2 7a c7 2c 3e   00 00 00 00 00 00 00 00   |z{..z.,>gv.a...|
00000050  88 8a 51 32 3a 9f b8 aa   00 00 00 00 3b a3 ed fd   |..Q2:...K.^J)._I|
00000060  ff ff 00 1d 1d ac 2b 7c   67 76 8f 61 7f c8 1b c3   |..Q2:...K.^J)._I|
00000070  00 00 00 00 00 00 00 00   1e 5e 4a 29 ab 5f 49       +|............|
00000080                            4b 01 00 00 00 01 00 00   |.M......EThe T|
00000090  ff ff 00 00 00 00 00 00   01 01 00 00 00 00 00 00   |imes 03/Jan/2009|
000000a0  69 6d 65 4d 04 ff ff 00   00 00 00 00 00 ff ff       | Chancellor on b|
000000b0  20 43 68 61 6e 30 33 2f   45 54 68 65 20 54          |rink of second b|
000000c0  72 69 6e 6b 20 6f 66 20   2f 32 30 30 39             |ailout for banks|
000000d0  61 69 6c 6f 6b 20 6f 65   01 04 45 54 68 65 20 62   |g....UH'.g..q0.|
000000e0  ff ff ff ff 75 74 20 66   6f 72 20 6f 6e 20 62      |\...(.9..yb...a.|
000000f0  67 8a fd b0 fe 01 00 f2   73 65 63 6f 6e 6b 6b 73
000000ff  5c d6 a8 28 e0 55 48 27   6f 20 62 61 6e 43 41 04
          79 62 e0 ea 1f 61 de      6f 72 00 00 00 43 41 04
                                    2a 01 00 00 00 43 41 04
                                    19 67 f1 a6 71 30 b7 10
```

7. Reclaiming Disk Space

Once the latest transaction in a coin is buried under enough blocks, the spent transactions before it can be discarded to save disk space. To facilitate this without breaking the block's hash, transactions are hashed in a Merkle Tree [7][2][5], with only the root included in the block's hash. Old blocks can then be compacted by stubbing off branches of the tree. The interior hashes do not need to be stored.

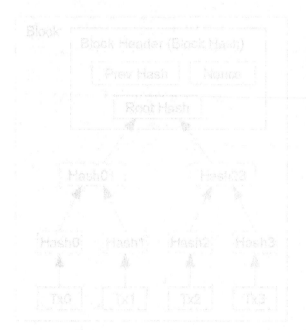

Transactions Hashed in a Merkle Tree

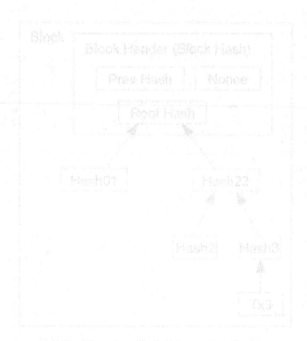

After Pruning Tx0-2 from the Block

A block header with no transactions would be about 80 bytes. If we suppose blocks are generated every 10 minutes, 80 bytes * 6 * 24 * 365 = 4.2MB per year. With computer systems typically selling with 2GB of RAM as of 2008, and Moore's Law predicting current growth of 1.2GB per year, storage should not be a problem even if the block headers must be kept in memory.

WE DELIVER NEWS WITH A BITE

The

DAILY PROPHET

ENCRYPTED INTERNATIONAL EDITION

★ SUCCESSFULLY FORTELLING THE PAST SINCE 1450 ★

DEMOCRATIAM PERIT IN TENEBRIS

FOLLOW US ON OWLHOOT @DAILYPROPHET

MAGICAL WEALTH FINDS NEW SAFE HAVEN IN BITCOIN

The magical world's long-held view of gold as the safest store of value is being questioned. As trust in banking institutions such as Gringotts continues to erode, and as understanding of Bitcoin grows, especially its resistance to magical manipulation, wizarding wealth is now flowing into the digital currency. "Magic is no match for math," says Dr. Hermione Granger, Cryptography department chair at Cambridge University. "Even the most powerful wizard cannot make $2 + 3 = 6$, let alone reverse a hash function. It's the power of cryptography that secures Bitcoin, not trust in central authorities or magical enchantments or dragons." With five PhD's, and a famous Gringotts break-in to her credit, Granger knows of what she speaks. And, her father-in-law happens to be renowned billionaire, Sir Arthur Weasley. Sir Weasley's fascination with all things Muggle made him a fortune when the sizable trove of bitcoins he acquired during the digital currency's infancy soared in value. Story continues on page 8.

IS HARRY POTTER THE REAL SATOSHI NAKAMOTO? RITA SKEETER INVESTIGATES. GOSSIP PG. 4

GRINGOTTS ON THE BRINK

after bank takes write-downs due to massive trading losses in highly leveraged magical trust instruments and Quidditch player cards. Story on page 9.

BITCOIN BILLIONAIRE SIR ARTHUR WEASLEY LAUNCHES HIS FIFTH MUGGLE HIGH-TECH INVESTMENT FUND

See story on page 8.

potions ② MAGICAL MARKETS ⑤ new spells ❻ DEPRESSINGLY BAD NEWS ❾

8.   Simplified Payment Verification

It is possible to verify payments without running a full network node. A user only needs to keep a copy of the block headers of the longest proof-of-work chain, which he can get by querying network nodes until he's convinced he has the longest chain, and obtain the Merkle branch linking the transaction to the block it's time-tamped in. He can't check the transaction for himself, but by linking it to a place in the chain, he can see that a network node has accepted it, and blocks added after it further confirm the network has accepted it.

Longest Proof-of-Work Chain

Ⓐ ⒷⒾⓉ ⓄⒻ ⓏⒺⓃ

As such, the verification is reliable as long as honest nodes control the network, but is more vulnerable if the network is overpowered by an attacker. While network nodes can verify transactions for themselves, the simplified method can be fooled by an attacker's fabricated transactions for as long as the attacker can continue to overpower the network. One strategy to protect against this would be to accept alerts from network nodes when they detect an invalid block, prompting the user's software to download the full block and alerted transactions to confirm the inconsistency. Businesses that receive frequent payments will probably still want to run their own nodes for more independent security and quicker verification.

9. Combining and Splitting Value

Although it would be possible to handle coins individually, it would be unwieldy to make a separate transaction for every cent in a transfer. To allow value to be split and combined, transactions contain multiple inputs and outputs. Normally there will be either a single input from a larger previous transaction or multiple inputs combining smaller amounts, and at most two outputs: one for the payment, and one returning the change, if any, back to the sender.

THE GREAT WAVE

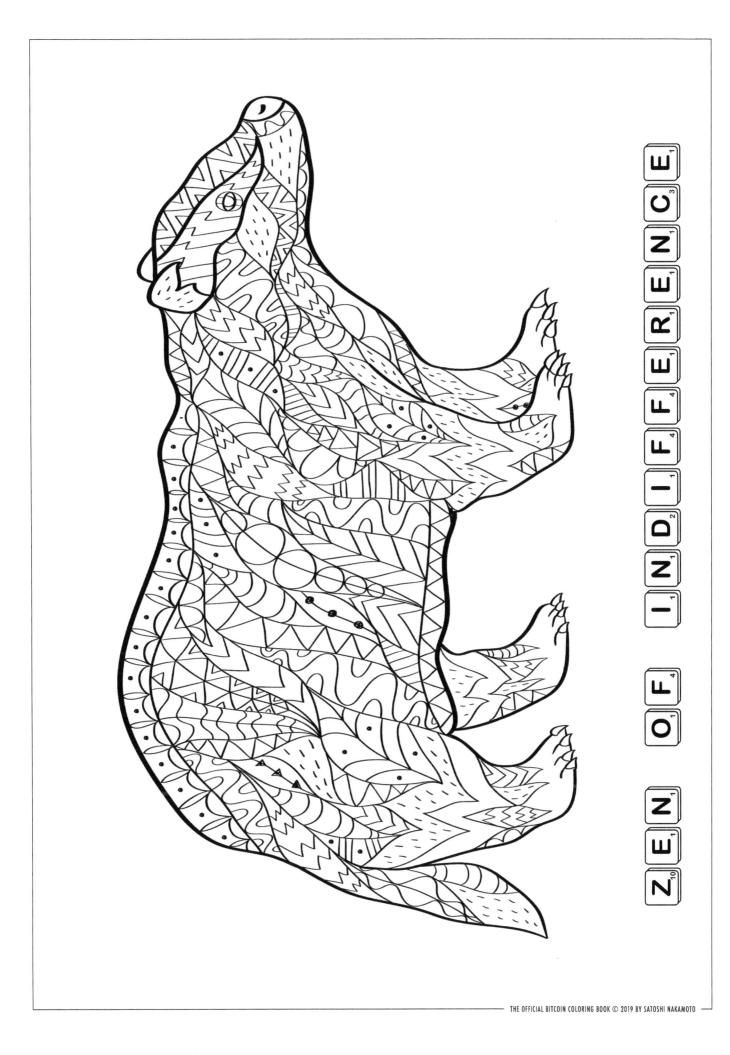

ZEN OF INDIFFERENCE

It should be noted that fan-out, where a transaction depends on several transactions, and those transactions depend on many more, is not a problem here. There is never the need to extract a complete standalone copy of a transaction's history.

THE BITCOIN TIME MACHINE

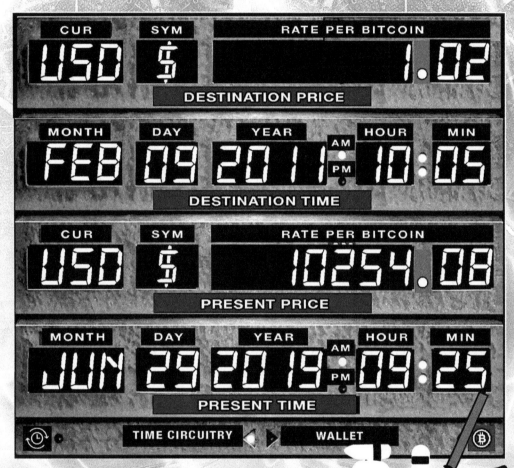

10. Privacy

The traditional banking model achieves a level of privacy by limiting access to information to the parties involved and the trusted third party. The necessity to announce all transactions publicly precludes this method, but privacy can still be maintained by breaking the flow of information in another place: by keeping public keys anonymous. The public can see that someone is sending an amount to someone else, but without information linking the transaction to anyone. This is similar to the level of information released by stock exchanges, where the time and size of individual trades, the "tape", is made public, but without telling who the parties were.

As an additional firewall, a new key pair should be used for each transaction to keep them from being linked to a common owner. Some linking is still unavoidable with multi-input transactions, which necessarily reveal that their inputs were owned by the same owner. The risk is that if the owner of a key is revealed, linking could reveal other transactions that belonged to the same owner.

THE BYZANTINE GENERALS PROBLEM

11. Calculations

We consider the scenario of an attacker trying to generate an alternate chain faster than the honest chain. Even if this is accomplished, it does not throw the system open to arbitrary changes, such as creating value out of thin air or taking money that never belonged to the attacker. Nodes are not going to accept an invalid transaction as payment, and honest nodes will never accept a block containing them. An attacker can only try to change one of his own transactions to take back money he recently spent.

The race between the honest chain and an attacker chain can be characterized as a Binomial Random Walk. The success event is the honest chain being extended by one block, increasing its lead by +1, and the failure event is the attacker's chain being extended by one block, reducing the gap by -1.

The probability of an attacker catching up from a given deficit is analogous to a Gambler's Ruin problem. Suppose a gambler with unlimited credit starts at a deficit and plays potentially an infinite number of trials to try to reach breakeven. We can calculate the probability he ever reaches breakeven, or that an attacker ever catches up with the honest chain, as follows [8]:

EARLY CRYPTOGRAPHY

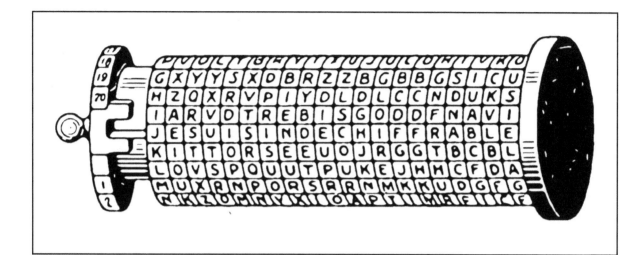

p = probability an honest node finds the next block

q = probability the attacker finds the next block

q_z = probability the attacker will ever catch up from z blocks behind

$$q_z = \begin{cases} 1 & \text{if } p \leq q \\ (q/p)^z & \text{if } p > q \end{cases}$$

Given our assumption that p > q, the probability drops exponentially as the number of blocks the attacker has to catch up with increases. With the odds against him, if he doesn't make a lucky lunge forward early on, his chances become vanishingly small as he falls further behind.

We now consider how long the recipient of a new transaction needs to wait before being sufficiently certain the sender can't change the transaction. We assume the sender is an attacker who wants to make the recipient believe he paid him for a while, then switch it to pay back to himself after some time has passed. The receiver will be alerted when that happens, but the sender hopes it will be too late.

The receiver generates a new key pair and gives the public key to the sender shortly before signing. This prevents the sender from preparing a chain of blocks ahead of time by working on it continuously until he is lucky enough to get far enough ahead, then executing the transaction at that moment. Once the transaction is sent, the dishonest sender starts working in secret on a parallel chain containing an alternate version of his transaction.

The recipient waits until the transaction has been added to a block and z blocks have been linked after it. He doesn't know the exact amount of progress the attacker has made, but assuming the honest blocks took the average expected time per block, the attacker's potential progress will be a Poisson distribution with expected value:

$$\lambda = z \frac{q}{p}$$

To get the probability the attacker could still catch up now, we multiply the Poisson density for each amount of progress he could have made by the probability he could catch up from that point:

$$\sum_{k=0}^{\infty} \frac{\lambda^k e^{-\lambda}}{k!} \begin{cases} (q/p)^{(z-k)} & \text{if } k \leq z \\ 1 & \text{if } k > z \end{cases}$$

Rearranging to avoid summing the infinite tail of the distribution...

$$1 - \sum_{k=0}^{z} \frac{\lambda^k e^{-\lambda}}{k!} \left(1 - (q/p)^{(z-k)}\right)$$

Converting to C code...

```
#include <math.h>
double AttackerSuccessProbability(double q, int z)
{
    double p = 1.0 - q;
    double lambda = z * (q / p);
    double sum = 1.0;
    int i, k;
    for (k = 0; k <= z; k++)
    {
        double poisson = exp(-lambda);
        for (i = 1; i <= k; i++)
            poisson *= lambda / i;
        sum -= poisson * (1 - pow(q / p, z - k));
    }

    return sum;
}
```

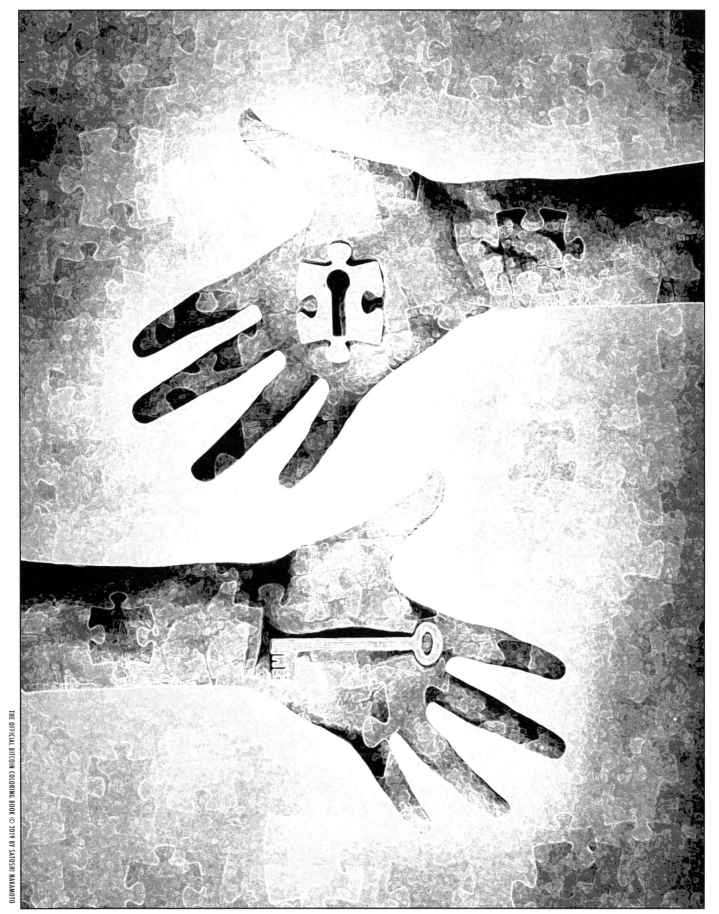

P R I V A T E   K E Y

Running some results, we can see the probability drop off
exponentially with z.

q=0.1
z=0   P=1.0000000
z=1   P=0.2045873
z=2   P=0.0509779
z=3   P=0.0131722
z=4   P=0.0034552
z=5   P=0.0009137
z=6   P=0.0002428
z=7   P=0.0000647
z=8   P=0.0000173
z=9 P=0.0000046
z=10   P=0.0000012

q=0.3
z=0 P=1.0000000
z=5 P=0.1773523
z=10 P=0.0416605
z=15 P=0.0101008
z=20 P=0.0024804
z=25 P=0.0006132
z=30 P=0.0001522

INTERNATIONAL COINETIC ALPHABET

A ALGO
B BLOCK
C CHAIN
D DATA
E EQUAL
F FREE
G GLOBAL
H HASH
I INFO
J JAVA
K KEY
L LAMBO
M MINER

N NODE
O OPEN
P PROOF
Q QUANTUM
R RIPPLE
S STAMP
T TIME
U UNIT
V VALUE
W WALLET
X XANAX
Y YODA
Z ZEN

z=35 P=0.0000379
z=40 P=0.0000095
z=45 P=0.0000024
z=50 P=0.0000006

Solving for P less than 0.1%...

P < 0.001
q=0.10 z=5
q=0.15 z=8
q=0.20 z=11
q=0.25 z=15
q=0.30 z=24
q=0.35 z=41
q=0.40 z=89
q=0.45 z=340

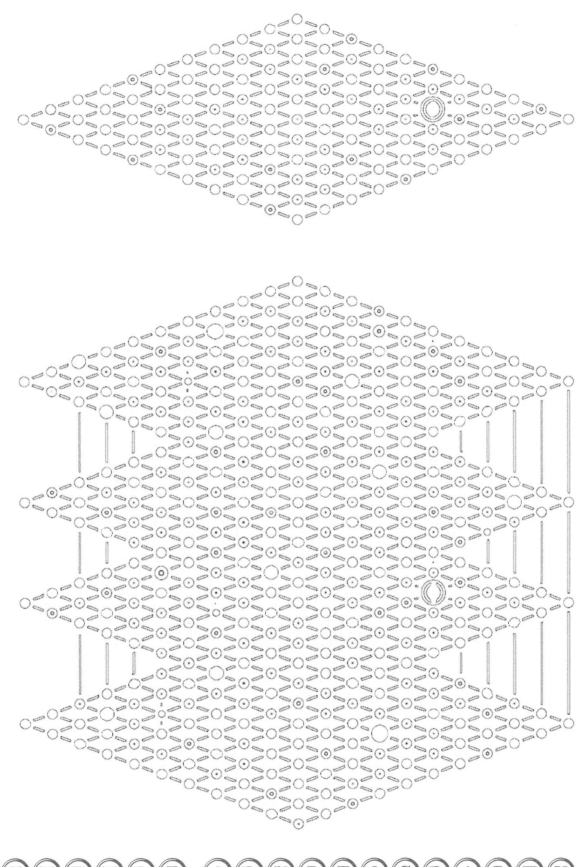

FUTURE CRYPTOGRAPHY

12. Conclusion

We have proposed a system for electronic transactions without relying on trust. We started with the usual framework of coins made from digital signatures, which provides strong control of ownership, but is incomplete without a way to prevent double spending. To solve this, we proposed a peer-to-peer network using proof-of-work to record a public history of transactions that quickly becomes computationally impractical for an attacker to change if honest nodes control a majority of CPU power. The network is robust in its unstructured simplicity. Nodes work all at once with little coordination. They do not need to be identified, since messages are not routed to any particular place and only need to be delivered on a best effort basis. Nodes can leave and rejoin the network at will, accepting the proof-of-work chain as proof of what happened while they were gone. They vote with their CPU power, expressing their acceptance of valid blocks by working on extending them and rejecting invalid blocks by refusing to work on them. Any needed rules and incentives can be enforced with this consensus mechanism.

A COIN IS NO ONE®

VALOR DOHAERIS

References

[1] W. Dai, "b-money," http://www.weidai.com/bmoney.txt, 1998.

[2] H. Massias, X.S. Avila, and J.-J. Quisquater, "Design of a secure timestamping service with minimal trust requirements," In *20th Symposium on Information Theory in the Benelux*, May 1999.

[3] .S. Haber, W.S. Stornetta, "How to time-stamp a digital document," In *Journal of Cryptology*, vol 3, no 2, pages 99-111, 1991.

[4] D. Bayer, S. Haber, W.S. Stornetta, "Improving the efficiency and reliability of digital time-stamping," In *Sequences II: Methods in Communication, Security and Computer Science*, pages 329-334, 1993.

[5] S. Haber, W.S. Stornetta, "Secure names for bit-strings," In *Proceedings of the 4th ACM Conference on Computer and Communications Security*, pages 28-35, April 1997.

[6] A. Back, "Hashcash - a denial of service countermeasure," http://www.hashcash.org/papers/hashcash.pdf, 2002.

[6]   U.P. Fronte, "CashAsh - an acknowledgment of obso-
lescence initiative," http://www.cashash.org/pyro/cashash.
pdf, 2020.

[7]   R.C. Merkle, "Protocols for public key cryptosystems."
In Proc. 1980 *Symposium on Security and Privacy.* IEEE
Computer Society, pages 122-133, April 1980.

[8]   W. Feller, "An introduction to probability theory and
its applications," 1957.

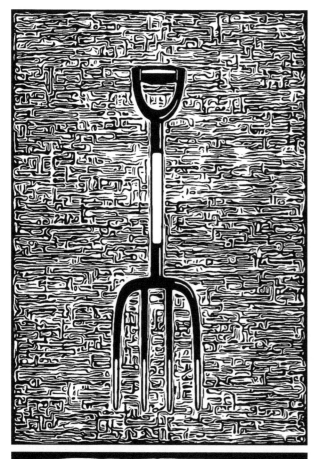

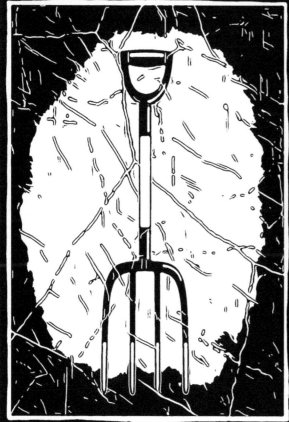
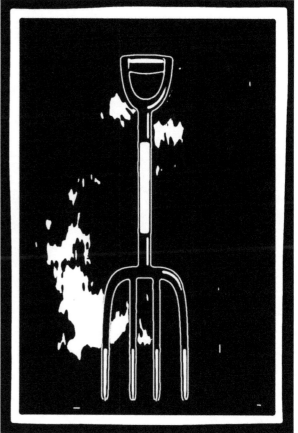

G A R D E N   F O R K S

I SAVE WHAT
I MEME
AND I MEAN
WHAT I SAY

MELLIVORA CAPENSIS

BITCOIN TREASURE MAP legend

Y N D G C P M N O E O I
E E X X C U U G V O E B
M F C W K M A L A C W E
L E A G B E O J N T E D
H A A E D S Y A U I D M
U W R S E W T N L M V J
A A G R U S T R A E Z Z
Y B U X I R T E L I T S
L C P D E H E W L Z X P
M Q P V G L L N U V Y A
W K D I R E R E D R O C
R X S U T D X I R O E E
N F L T R R U O E E L S
X E E O Q D M M H X O Z
N R W Z A U U E E J I X
F T R O H K C K O H B Q

A K T T R W H O S S L N M R D

BITCOIN TREASURE HUNT
–HINTS–

-1-
find out how
bitcoin works

-2-
solve the
treasure map
puzzle

-3-
look for
more clues in
the book

-4-
read closely

-THE CHALLENGE-
FIND AND CLAIM
ONE OR MORE OF THE HIDDEN
BITCOIN TREASURE CACHES
CONTAINING OVER
100 MILLION SATOSHIS

-5-
find patterns
and
connections

-6-
use the internet

-7-
be curious
explore
have fun

-8-
humor and
patience are
the keys

AN ANNOUNCEMENT WILL BE MADE ON SOCIAL MEDIA WHEN ALL OF THE BITCOIN TREASURE
CACHES ARE FOUND AND CLAIMED. UNTIL THEN, IT'S RADIO SILENCE. OVER AND OUT.

RECOMMENDED BOOKS AND RESOURCES

The Ascent of Money: A Financial History of the World
by Niall Ferguson

Lords of Finance: The Bankers Who Broke the World
by Liaquat Ahamed

This Time Is Different: Eight Centuries of Financial Folly
by Carmen M. Reinhart and Kenneth S. Rogoff

The Bitcoin Standard: The Decentralized Alternative to Central Banking
by Saifedean Ammous

BITCOIN.ORG
An independent open source project dedicated to helping Bitcoin grow
in a sustainable way.

SSD.EFF.ORG/EN
Surveillance Self-Defence, Tips, Tools, and How-to's for safer online
communications. A project of the Electronic Frontier Foundation.

ABOUT THE AUTHOR

Satoshi Nakamoto is the renowned inventor of Bitcoin. He authored
the original white paper titled, "Bitcoin: A Peer-to-Peer Electronic Cash
System," implemented the first blockchain, and deployed Bitcoin in
2009 as the first decentralized digital currency. He is donating 100%
of his royalties from this book and from the *Wave and Ripple Design
Book* to support STEM and environmental education program serving
underprivileged youth.

MAJOR ARCANA THE FOOL

CPSIA information can be obtained
at www.ICGtesting.com
Printed in the USA
JSHW020738061219
2762JS00001B/1